Boost Your Team's Speed

Quick and Easy Ways to Get Things Done Faster

By Mohammad Zaripour

Copyright

© 2024 Mohammad Zaripour. All rights reserved.

No part of this book may be reproduced, distributed, or transmitted in any form or by any means, including photocopying, recording, or other electronic or mechanical methods, without the prior written permission of the publisher, except in the case of brief quotations embodied in critical reviews and certain other noncommercial uses permitted by copyright law.

Published by KDP Kindle Direct Publishing

About the Author

Mohammad Zaripour is a seasoned professional with a rich background in project management and engineering. His extensive experience is bolstered by prestigious certifications, including Project Management Professional (PMP), PMI Agile Certified Practitioner (PMI-ACP), Professional Scrum Master (PSM), and Engineer-in-Training (EIT). These credentials underscore his commitment to excellence and his continuous pursuit of knowledge.

With a career that spans multiple industries, Mohammad has expertly applied his project management and engineering skills to drive complex projects to successful completion. His approach combines meticulous planning, effective communication, and a focus on quality, drawing from both traditional and agile methodologies.

Table of Content

Introduction 8
Chapter 1 12
Chapter 2 26
Chapter 3 39
Chapter 4 53
Chapter 5 66
Chapter 6 79
Chapter 7 92
Chapter 8 105
Conclusion 118
Appendix 123
References 131

Abstract:

In today's fast-paced world, the ability to execute tasks quickly and efficiently can make all the difference between success and failure. "Boost Your Team's Speed: Quick and Easy Ways to Get Things Done Faster" is a practical guide designed to help teams enhance their performance and accelerate their execution speed. This book delves into straightforward strategies and techniques that can be implemented immediately to see real improvements in productivity.

Drawing from years of experience and expertise, this book offers insights into creating a cohesive team environment where everyone is motivated and empowered to perform at their best. It covers essential topics such as effective communication, prioritization, and time management, all presented in a clear and engaging manner. The book also highlights the importance of maintaining a positive and fun workplace culture, which can significantly impact the overall efficiency and satisfaction of the team.

With a touch of humor and relatable examples, "Boost Your Team's Speed" provides valuable advice for leaders and team members alike, making it an enjoyable and informative read. Whether you're a seasoned manager or just starting out, this book will equip you with the tools and knowledge needed to transform your team into a high-speed, high-performing unit.

Introduction

Introduction

Welcome to "Boost Your Team's Speed: Quick and Easy Ways to Get Things Done Faster." In the hustle and bustle of today's business world, where deadlines are tight and expectations high, the ability to execute tasks swiftly and efficiently has never been more crucial. Whether you're a seasoned manager or just beginning your journey as a team leader, this book is designed to equip you with the tools and insights needed to significantly enhance your team's performance.

Let's start by exploring the concept of execution speed. Execution speed is not just about doing things quickly; it's about doing them efficiently and effectively, without compromising on quality. It involves streamlining processes, optimizing workflows, and ensuring that every team member is aligned and motivated to achieve common goals. When a team operates at high speed, it can respond faster to changes, seize opportunities promptly, and deliver outstanding results consistently.

In today's fast-paced business environment, speed is more than just a competitive advantage; it's a necessity. Companies that can execute rapidly are better positioned to meet customer demands, adapt to market shifts, and stay ahead of the competition. Speed enables businesses to be agile, resilient, and responsive, which are essential qualities in a world where the only constant is change. The ability to execute quickly can be the difference between thriving and merely surviving.

In this book, you will learn practical strategies and techniques to boost your team's execution speed. We will delve into topics such as effective communication, prioritization, and time management, providing you with actionable advice that can be implemented immediately. You'll discover how to create a culture of accountability, trust, and empowerment within your team, which are critical components for achieving high-speed execution. We'll explore the importance of leveraging technology and tools to automate repetitive tasks and streamline workflows, ensuring that your team can focus on what truly matters.

Moreover, we will discuss how to foster a collaborative environment where teamwork flourishes, and how to maintain momentum by keeping your team motivated and engaged. A significant part of our journey will also focus on the role of fun and positivity in enhancing productivity. You'll learn how to create a workplace culture that balances hard work with humor and enjoyment, leading to a happier, more efficient team.

Throughout the book, you'll find a blend of insights drawn from years of experience, coupled with real-life examples and a touch of humor to keep things engaging. Our goal is to make this a valuable and enjoyable read, providing you with the knowledge and inspiration needed to transform your team into a high-speed, high-performing unit.

So, buckle up and get ready to turbocharge your team's execution speed. By the end of this book, you'll be equipped with a comprehensive toolkit to help your team get things done faster and more efficiently, all while having a bit of fun along the way. Let's embark on this exciting journey together and unlock the full potential of your team's speed and efficiency.

Chapter 1

Chapter 1

Understanding Execution Speed

In the quest to enhance your team's productivity and efficiency, the first step is to understand what we mean by "execution speed." It's a term that's often tossed around in business meetings and management seminars, but what does it truly entail? Execution speed is about more than just working quickly; it's about working smartly, effectively, and with a clear purpose.

Execution speed encompasses the ability to carry out tasks promptly while maintaining a high standard of quality. It involves minimizing delays, eliminating unnecessary steps, and ensuring that every team member is working harmoniously towards common objectives. A team with high execution speed can adapt swiftly to changes, capitalize on opportunities as they arise, and deliver results that exceed expectations.

Defining Execution Speed

Let's break down the concept further. Execution speed is the efficiency and effectiveness with which a team completes its tasks. It's about streamlining processes so that each step adds value and moves the team closer to its goals. This means having clear workflows, defined roles and responsibilities, and a keen focus on eliminating bottlenecks that slow down progress. Imagine a race car pit crew, where every member knows their role and performs with precision and speed. Just like in a pit stop, a team's execution speed can determine the outcome of the race.

One common misconception is that speed sacrifices quality. This is not the case when execution speed is properly managed. The goal is to maintain or even improve quality while reducing the time taken to achieve it. It's about being agile, where the team can pivot and adjust its approach without losing momentum. Think of a well-rehearsed dance troupe; they move quickly and gracefully, yet every step is executed perfectly.

The Benefits of Increased Execution Speed

Why is it so important to focus on execution speed? The benefits are manifold and can significantly impact both the short-term and long-term success of your team and organization.

First and foremost, increased execution speed enhances productivity. When a team can complete tasks quickly and efficiently, it can take on more projects and deliver results more frequently. This not only boosts the overall output but also allows the team to meet tight deadlines and manage multiple priorities effectively. Consider a fast-food kitchen during peak hours, where speed and efficiency are paramount to keeping customers satisfied.

A faster execution speed also provides a competitive edge. In a business landscape where time is often a critical factor, being able to deliver products or services quicker than competitors can be a decisive advantage. It allows companies to respond to market demands promptly, launch new products faster, and provide superior customer service. For example, tech companies that can quickly adapt and innovate are often the ones that lead the market.

Furthermore, a team that executes swiftly and efficiently tends to have higher morale and job satisfaction. When team members see the tangible results of their hard work and feel a sense of accomplishment, it fosters a positive and motivated work environment. This, in turn, leads to increased engagement and a stronger commitment to the team's goals. Imagine a sports team that works together seamlessly to win a championship; the sense of achievement and camaraderie is palpable.

Common Misconceptions about Speed and Productivity

It's important to address some of the common misconceptions surrounding execution speed. One major misconception is that working faster means cutting corners or compromising on quality. In reality, true execution speed is about optimizing processes and eliminating inefficiencies, not about rushing through tasks without regard for quality. It's about working smarter, not harder.

Another misconception is that increasing speed will inevitably lead to burnout. While it's true that overworking can cause burnout, the strategies we'll explore in this book focus on working smarter, not harder. By prioritizing tasks effectively, leveraging technology, and fostering a supportive team environment, we can increase speed without overwhelming the team. It's akin to training for a marathon; pacing and strategy are key to avoiding exhaustion and achieving peak performance.

Personal Story: The Tale of Two Projects

Let me share a personal story to illustrate these points. A few years ago, I was leading two different project teams in my organization. The first team struggled with execution speed. Despite their hard work, they often missed deadlines and faced quality issues. They were constantly firefighting, trying to keep up with the demands. Morale was low, and stress levels were high.

The second team, however, had a different approach. We focused on streamlining processes, clear communication, and leveraging technology. Tasks were prioritized, and responsibilities were clearly defined. The team was empowered to make decisions, and we fostered a culture of trust and accountability. The results were remarkable. Not only did we complete projects ahead of schedule, but the quality of work was also exceptional. The team was motivated and proud of their achievements, which created a positive and productive work environment.

Including Data and Statistics

To support the importance of execution speed, consider the following statistics: According to a study by McKinsey & Company, organizations that prioritize speed are twice as likely to achieve above-average revenue growth and profitability. Another report by Bain & Company found that companies with high-speed decision-making processes are 20% more likely to outperform their competitors. These figures underscore the critical role that execution speed plays in driving business success.

Thought-Provoking Questions

As you think about execution speed, consider these questions: What processes in your team are causing delays? How can you streamline workflows to eliminate bottlenecks? Are there tasks that can be automated to free up time for more important activities? Reflecting on these questions can help you identify areas for improvement and set the stage for implementing the strategies discussed in this book.

Exercises and Activities

At the end of this chapter, take some time to conduct a team exercise. Gather your team and map out your current workflows. Identify any steps that are redundant or time-consuming. Discuss ways to optimize these processes and set clear, actionable goals for improvement. This exercise can provide valuable insights and foster a sense of collaboration and ownership among team members.

Analogies and Metaphors

Think of execution speed as a river flowing towards its destination. A smooth, unobstructed flow ensures that the water reaches its goal quickly and efficiently. However, if there are rocks and debris in the river, the flow is disrupted, causing delays and inefficiencies. Your role as a leader is to remove these obstacles and ensure a clear path for your team.

Case Studies

To illustrate the power of improving execution speed, let's delve into some real-world examples of companies that have successfully accelerated their operations. One notable example is **Amazon**. Amazon is renowned for its efficiency and rapid delivery times, which are crucial to its success. The company has implemented advanced logistics and supply chain management systems to streamline operations. Amazon's use of robotics in its warehouses, along with sophisticated inventory management systems, allows it to process orders quickly and accurately. The result is a highly efficient delivery network that sets the standard for e-commerce.

Another example is **Toyota**, which is known for its lean manufacturing system, the Toyota Production System (TPS). TPS focuses on eliminating waste and improving efficiency through techniques like Just-In-Time production and continuous improvement (Kaizen). By implementing these strategies, Toyota has been able to reduce production times and costs while maintaining high-quality standards. The company's success demonstrates how focusing on speed and efficiency can lead to significant competitive advantages.

Tools and Technologies

Various tools and technologies can greatly enhance execution speed by streamlining workflows and improving efficiency. **Project management software** like **Asana** or **Trello** helps teams organize tasks, track progress, and collaborate effectively. These platforms allow for clear task assignments, deadlines, and status updates, ensuring everyone is aligned and tasks are completed on time.

Communication platforms such as **Slack** or **Microsoft Teams** are essential for maintaining fast and efficient communication within teams. These tools facilitate real-time messaging, file sharing, and video conferencing, reducing the time spent on back-and-forth emails and meetings.

Automation tools like **Zapier** or **Integromat** can automate repetitive tasks and workflows, freeing up time for more strategic activities. For instance, you can set up automated workflows to handle routine data entry, notifications, or file management, reducing manual effort and minimizing errors.

Leadership and Execution Speed

Leadership plays a pivotal role in fostering a culture that values speed and efficiency. Effective leaders set the tone for their teams by modeling swift decision-making and encouraging a results-driven mindset. **Elon Musk**, CEO of SpaceX and Tesla, is a prime example of a leader who emphasizes speed. His approach involves setting ambitious goals and creating an environment where rapid execution is expected and celebrated.

Leaders can also motivate their teams by clearly communicating the vision and goals, providing the necessary resources, and removing obstacles that hinder progress. Implementing practices such as regular check-ins, feedback sessions, and recognition programs can help maintain high levels of motivation and performance. Encouraging a culture of accountability and ownership, where team members take responsibility for their tasks and outcomes, further enhances execution speed.

Measuring Execution Speed

Measuring execution speed involves tracking various metrics to assess how efficiently tasks and projects are completed. One key method is to use **Key Performance Indicators (KPIs)** such as cycle time, which measures the time taken to complete a task from start to finish. Another important metric is **lead time**, which tracks the total time from receiving a request to delivering the final product or service.

Teams can also use **project tracking tools** to monitor progress against deadlines and milestones. For example, Gantt charts or Kanban boards can visually represent task completion and workflow efficiency. Regularly reviewing these metrics helps teams identify bottlenecks, assess performance, and set benchmarks for continuous improvement.

Overcoming Challenges

Improving execution speed often involves addressing several common challenges. One significant challenge is **resistance to change**. Teams may be accustomed to established processes and may resist new methods or technologies. To overcome this, leaders should involve team members in the change process, provide training, and communicate the benefits of the new approach.

Another challenge is **managing workload**. Teams may face high-pressure situations with tight deadlines that can affect performance. Effective prioritization and time management strategies, along with the use of productivity tools, can help manage workload and maintain efficiency.

Maintaining **quality under tight deadlines** is another challenge. It's important to balance speed with quality by implementing quality control measures and ensuring that team members have the necessary resources and support to meet high standards.

Future Trends

The field of execution speed is continuously evolving, driven by advancements in technology and changes in work culture. **Artificial Intelligence (AI)** and **machine learning** are expected to play a significant role in automating complex tasks and optimizing workflows. AI-powered tools can analyze data, predict trends, and make recommendations, further enhancing execution speed.

Remote work and **distributed teams** are becoming more common, necessitating new tools and practices for maintaining efficiency across different locations. Technologies that support seamless collaboration and communication will be crucial in this evolving work environment.

Agile methodologies and **lean practices** will likely continue to influence how teams approach execution speed. These methodologies emphasize flexibility, iterative progress, and continuous improvement, which are essential for adapting to changing demands and achieving fast results.

Interactive Elements

To help readers evaluate and improve their execution speed, consider adding interactive elements such as:

- **Quizzes**: Assess current practices and identify areas for improvement.
- **Self-Assessment Tools**: Provide checklists or questionnaires to evaluate time management and efficiency.
- **Checklists**: Offer actionable steps to implement strategies for boosting execution speed.

These interactive tools can engage readers and provide personalized insights into their execution practices.

Expert Interviews

Including interviews with experts in productivity and efficiency can add depth and credibility to the content. For instance, an interview with a productivity consultant or a renowned project manager can provide valuable insights into successful strategies and real-world applications. Experts can share their experiences, discuss emerging trends, and offer practical advice on improving execution speed.

By incorporating these elements into Chapter 1, you can provide readers with a comprehensive understanding of how to enhance execution speed and apply practical strategies to their own work environments.

Understanding execution speed is the foundation upon which we will build throughout this book. By grasping what it truly means to execute tasks quickly and efficiently, and recognizing the immense benefits it brings, we set the stage for transforming our teams into high-speed, high-performing units. In the next chapters, we will delve into practical strategies and techniques to enhance execution speed, ensuring that your team can achieve remarkable results swiftly and effectively.

With a blend of practical advice, personal anecdotes, and thought-provoking insights, this book aims to be your guide to turbocharging your team's execution speed. So, let's embark on this exciting journey together and unlock the full potential of your team's speed and efficiency.

Chapter 2

Chapter 2

Setting the Stage for Speed

To enhance your team's execution speed, it's crucial to create the right environment and foundation. This involves cultivating a culture that prioritizes speed, establishing clear goals and expectations, and providing the necessary tools and resources. In this chapter, we'll explore how to set the stage for speed, ensuring that your team is poised for swift and efficient execution.

Creating a Culture of Speed

The first step in setting the stage for speed is to foster a culture that values and encourages rapid execution. This doesn't mean rushing through tasks haphazardly but rather instilling a mindset that emphasizes efficiency, agility, and continuous improvement. Creating a culture of speed starts with leadership. As a leader, you must model the behaviors and attitudes you want to see in your team. Show your commitment to speed by making swift decisions, addressing issues promptly, and continuously seeking ways to improve processes.

Encourage open communication and collaboration. When team members feel comfortable sharing ideas and feedback, it leads to faster problem-solving and innovation. Create an environment where everyone feels empowered to take initiative and make decisions. This not only speeds up execution but also fosters a sense of ownership and accountability.

Setting Clear Goals and Expectations

Clear goals and expectations are essential for rapid execution. When everyone on the team understands what needs to be done and why it needs to be done quickly, they are more likely to stay focused and motivated. Start by setting SMART goals—specific, measurable, achievable, relevant, and time-bound. These goals provide a clear roadmap and help prioritize tasks.

Communicate these goals and expectations clearly and consistently. Regularly review progress and provide feedback to ensure that everyone is aligned and on track. Use visual aids like charts and dashboards to make goals and progress visible to the entire team. This not only keeps everyone informed but also creates a sense of urgency and accountability.

Providing the Right Tools and Resources

To enhance execution speed, it's essential to equip your team with the right tools and resources. This includes both physical tools, like technology and equipment, and intangible resources, such as training and support. Invest in tools that streamline workflows and automate repetitive tasks. Project management software, communication platforms, and collaboration tools can significantly enhance efficiency and speed.

Provide ongoing training and development opportunities to ensure that team members have the skills and knowledge needed to perform their tasks quickly and effectively. Encourage continuous learning and stay updated with industry trends and best practices. By providing the necessary tools and resources, you enable your team to work more efficiently and maintain high execution speed.

Personal Story: The Power of Clear Goals

A few years ago, I led a team tasked with developing a new product within a tight deadline. Initially, the project was plagued by delays and confusion. Team members were unclear about their roles, and there was a lack of coordination. To address this, we organized a series of workshops to define clear goals and expectations. We broke down the project into smaller, manageable tasks and assigned specific responsibilities to each team member.

We also implemented a project management tool to track progress and ensure transparency. The results were remarkable. The team became more focused and motivated, and we were able to complete the project ahead of schedule. This experience reinforced the importance of clear goals and expectations in achieving high execution speed.

Incorporating Quotes and References

To emphasize the importance of setting the stage for speed, consider the words of management expert Peter Drucker: "Efficiency is doing things right; effectiveness is doing the right things." By creating a culture of speed, setting clear goals, and providing the right tools, we can ensure that our teams are both efficient and effective.

A study by the Harvard Business Review found that companies with a strong culture of speed are 52% more likely to outperform their competitors. This highlights the significant impact that a well-established foundation for speed can have on an organization's success.

Thought-Provoking Questions

As you think about setting the stage for speed, consider these questions: What aspects of your team's culture might be slowing down execution? How can you create a sense of urgency without causing undue stress? What tools and resources could enhance your team's efficiency? Reflecting on these questions can help you identify areas for improvement and create a solid foundation for speed.

Exercises and Activities

At the end of this chapter, conduct a team exercise to evaluate your current tools and resources. Gather feedback from team members on what works well and what could be improved. Discuss potential investments in new technology or training programs that could enhance efficiency. This exercise can provide valuable insights and help you prioritize initiatives to boost execution speed.

Analogies and Metaphors

Think of setting the stage for speed as preparing a race car for a high-stakes competition. You wouldn't send the car onto the track without ensuring it's in peak condition, with a well-tuned engine, high-quality tires, and a skilled driver. Similarly, you need to equip your team with the right tools, clear goals, and a supportive culture to ensure they can perform at their best.

Case Studies

To understand how to set the stage for speed, let's look at some real-world examples of organizations that have done this successfully. Take **Google** for instance. Google fosters a culture of innovation and speed by allowing employees to spend 20% of their time on projects they are passionate about. This policy encourages creativity and swift problem-solving, leading to groundbreaking developments like Gmail and Google Maps. By creating an environment where speed and innovation are valued, Google continuously evolves and stays ahead in the tech industry.

Another example is **Zappos**, an online shoe and clothing retailer. Zappos emphasizes a strong company culture and exceptional customer service. By empowering employees to make decisions and take actions without waiting for approval, Zappos ensures that customer issues are resolved quickly, enhancing customer satisfaction and loyalty. Their strategy of investing in employee training and maintaining an open, communicative environment has been key to their success in creating a fast-paced, responsive business model.

Tools and Technologies

Various tools and technologies can help create an environment conducive to speed. **Project management software** like **Jira** or **Monday.com** helps teams plan, track, and manage their work efficiently. These platforms provide clear visibility into tasks, deadlines, and project statuses, enabling teams to stay organized and move quickly.

Communication platforms such as **Slack** or **Zoom** are essential for maintaining fast and effective communication, especially in remote or distributed teams. These tools facilitate real-time messaging, video conferencing, and file sharing, reducing the time spent on emails and meetings.

Automation tools like **Zapier** or **Microsoft Power Automate** can automate repetitive tasks, such as data entry or email notifications, freeing up time for more strategic work. Automation reduces manual effort and minimizes errors, streamlining workflows and enhancing overall speed.

Leadership's Role

Leadership is crucial in driving a culture of speed. Leaders set the tone by making swift decisions and demonstrating the importance of quick, yet thoughtful, action. **Elon Musk**, CEO of SpaceX and Tesla, exemplifies this by setting ambitious goals and creating an environment where rapid execution is expected. His approach encourages teams to innovate and iterate quickly.

Leaders can also foster an environment of trust and accountability by empowering team members to take ownership of their tasks and make decisions. This reduces bottlenecks and enables faster execution. Regular communication, clear expectations, and recognition of achievements are key practices for leaders to maintain a high-speed culture.

Measuring Success

To measure the effectiveness of initiatives aimed at increasing speed, teams can use various metrics. **Key Performance Indicators (KPIs)** such as cycle time, which measures the time taken to complete a task from start to finish, are essential. Another important metric is **lead time**, tracking the total time from receiving a request to delivering the final product or service.

Regularly reviewing these metrics helps teams identify areas for improvement and set benchmarks for success. **Project tracking tools** like Gantt charts or Kanban boards can visually represent task completion and workflow efficiency, providing a clear picture of progress and areas needing attention.

Overcoming Resistance

Implementing a culture of speed often faces resistance, as people may be accustomed to established processes. To overcome this, leaders should involve team members in the change process, providing training and communicating the benefits of the new approach. Highlighting success stories and demonstrating quick wins can also help gain buy-in.

Addressing concerns and providing support during the transition period is crucial. Encouraging open dialogue and feedback allows team members to voice their concerns and feel heard, which can significantly reduce resistance to change.

Future Trends

Emerging trends and future developments are likely to impact how teams set the stage for speed. **Artificial Intelligence (AI)** and **machine learning** are expected to play a significant role in automating complex tasks and optimizing workflows. AI-powered tools can analyze data, predict trends, and make recommendations, further enhancing execution speed.

Remote work and **distributed teams** are becoming more common, necessitating new tools and practices for maintaining efficiency across different locations. Technologies that support seamless collaboration and communication will be crucial in this evolving work environment.

Agile methodologies and **lean practices** will likely continue to influence how teams approach execution speed. These methodologies emphasize flexibility, iterative progress, and continuous improvement, which are essential for adapting to changing demands and achieving fast results.

Interactive Elements

To help readers evaluate and improve their current environment for speed, consider adding interactive elements such as:

- **Self-Assessment Tools**: Provide questionnaires to evaluate current practices and identify areas for improvement.

- **Checklists**: Offer actionable steps to implement strategies for creating a fast-paced environment.

- **Quizzes**: Assess understanding and application of concepts discussed in the chapter.

These interactive tools can engage readers and provide personalized insights into their execution practices.

Expert Interviews

Including interviews with experts in productivity and efficiency can add depth and credibility to the content. For instance, an interview with a productivity consultant or a renowned project manager can provide valuable insights into successful strategies and real-world applications. Experts can share their experiences, discuss emerging trends, and offer practical advice on setting the stage for speed.

Setting the stage for speed is a critical step in enhancing your team's execution speed. By creating a culture that values speed, setting clear goals and expectations, and providing the necessary tools and resources, you lay the groundwork for swift and efficient execution. In the following chapters, we will delve into specific strategies and techniques to further enhance your team's speed and performance.

With a blend of practical advice, personal anecdotes, and thought-provoking insights, this book aims to be your guide to turbocharging your team's execution speed. So, let's continue this exciting journey together and unlock the full potential of your team's speed and efficiency.

Chapter 3

Chapter 3

Building a High-Speed Team

Once the foundation is set, the next crucial step is to build a team capable of executing tasks with remarkable speed and efficiency. This chapter delves into the key elements required to create such a team, including recruitment, training, motivation, and effective leadership.

Recruiting the Right Talent

The journey to building a high-speed team begins with recruiting the right talent. It's essential to look for individuals who not only possess the necessary skills but also share the team's values and commitment to speed. When recruiting, prioritize candidates who demonstrate agility, problem-solving abilities, and a proactive mindset. These traits are invaluable in a fast-paced environment where adaptability and quick thinking are crucial.

Consider the case of a tech startup I worked with a few years ago. The company prioritized hiring candidates who could thrive in a dynamic, high-pressure environment. They sought out individuals who were not only technically proficient but also exhibited strong collaborative skills and a willingness to learn. This approach enabled the company to assemble a team that could innovate rapidly and respond swiftly to market changes, giving them a significant competitive edge.

Training and Development

Recruitment is just the beginning. To build a high-speed team, continuous training and development are essential. Invest in regular training sessions that focus on both technical skills and soft skills such as communication, time management, and teamwork. Encourage a culture of continuous learning where team members are motivated to keep improving and staying updated with industry trends.

A study by the Association for Talent Development found that companies with comprehensive training programs experience 24% higher profit margins than those that spend less on training. This underscores the importance of investing in your team's development. For example, implementing a mentorship program where experienced team members guide newer employees can accelerate the learning process and enhance overall team performance.

Motivation and Engagement

A motivated and engaged team is more likely to execute tasks quickly and effectively. Understanding what drives your team members and providing the right incentives is key to maintaining high levels of motivation. This can include financial rewards, recognition, opportunities for career advancement, and a positive work environment.

Personalizing motivation strategies can make a significant difference. In my previous role as a project manager, I implemented a recognition program where team members could nominate their peers for outstanding contributions. This not only boosted morale but also fostered a sense of camaraderie and teamwork. By acknowledging and rewarding hard work, you create a positive feedback loop that encourages continued high performance.

Effective Leadership

Leadership plays a pivotal role in building and maintaining a high-speed team. Effective leaders inspire their teams, set clear expectations, and provide the support needed to overcome obstacles. They lead by example, demonstrating the importance of speed and efficiency through their actions.

One of the most effective leadership styles for fostering speed is transformational leadership. Transformational leaders inspire and motivate their teams by creating a compelling vision and fostering a sense of purpose. They empower team members to take ownership of their work and encourage innovation and creative problem-solving.

Case Study: The Transformational Leader

Consider the case of a manufacturing company struggling with slow production times. The new CEO, a transformational leader, implemented several changes to turn things around. She began by setting a clear vision for the company's future, emphasizing the importance of speed and efficiency. She empowered team leaders to make decisions and encouraged open communication and collaboration across departments.

The CEO also introduced a series of training programs to enhance skills and foster a culture of continuous improvement. Within a year, the company saw a significant reduction in production times and an increase in overall productivity. This transformation was attributed to the CEO's leadership style and her ability to inspire and motivate the team.

Quotes and References

As renowned management consultant and author Tom Peters once said, "Leaders don't create followers, they create more leaders." This quote encapsulates the essence of effective leadership in building a high-speed team. By empowering and inspiring your team members, you create a culture where speed and efficiency thrive.

A report by Gallup found that teams with high engagement levels show 21% greater profitability. This highlights the direct correlation between motivation, engagement, and business success, further emphasizing the importance of these elements in building a high-speed team.

Thought-Provoking Questions

Consider these questions as you reflect on building your high-speed team: What qualities do you prioritize when recruiting new team members? How can you enhance your current training programs to foster continuous learning? What strategies can you implement to motivate and engage your team more effectively? Reflecting on these questions can help you identify areas for improvement and implement effective strategies to build a high-speed team.

Exercises and Activities

Conduct a team-building exercise focused on collaboration and problem-solving. Present a challenging scenario and have team members work together to find a solution. This not only fosters teamwork but also provides insights into each member's strengths and how they can be leveraged to enhance execution speed.

Analogies and Metaphors

Building a high-speed team is akin to assembling a championship sports team. You need the right players with the right skills, continuous training and practice, and a coach who can inspire and guide the team to victory. Just as a sports team thrives on collaboration, strategy, and motivation, so too does a high-speed business team.

Case Studies

To understand how to build high-speed teams, let's look at real-world examples of organizations that have done this successfully. **Netflix** is a prime example. Netflix has a unique culture that prioritizes freedom and responsibility. They hire top talent and give employees the freedom to make decisions, encouraging innovation and speed. Their recruitment strategy focuses on finding individuals who thrive in a fast-paced, constantly changing environment. Netflix's training programs are minimal; instead, they rely on hiring experienced professionals who can hit the ground running.

Another example is **Toyota**. Toyota's team-building approach, known as the Toyota Production System, emphasizes continuous improvement and respect for people. Their recruitment strategy includes rigorous training programs that focus on lean manufacturing principles and teamwork. Toyota encourages employees at all levels to suggest improvements, fostering a culture where everyone is engaged in speeding up processes and eliminating waste.

Tools and Technologies

Various tools and technologies can support the development of a high-speed team. **Collaboration**

platforms like **Microsoft Teams** or **Slack** facilitate real-time communication and collaboration, ensuring that team members can quickly share information and coordinate efforts.

Project management software such as **Asana** or **Trello** helps teams organize their work, set priorities, and track progress. These tools provide visibility into tasks and deadlines, enabling teams to work more efficiently and stay on track.

Training resources like **LinkedIn Learning** or **Coursera** offer a wealth of courses that can help team members develop new skills and stay updated with the latest industry trends. Continuous learning is crucial for maintaining high-speed teams that can adapt to new challenges and technologies.

Leadership Styles

Different leadership styles can significantly impact team speed and efficiency. **Transformational leadership** focuses on inspiring and motivating team members to exceed their expectations. Transformational leaders encourage innovation and creativity, which can lead to faster and more effective problem-solving. They build a vision and guide their teams towards it, fostering a high-speed, high-performance culture.

Transactional leadership, on the other hand, is more focused on structured tasks and rewards. It relies on clear roles and responsibilities, offering rewards for meeting specific goals. While this style can ensure efficiency and clarity, it might not inspire the same level of innovation and speed as transformational leadership.

Servant leadership emphasizes supporting and empowering team members. Servant leaders prioritize the needs of their team, providing resources and removing obstacles to help them succeed. This approach can build strong, motivated teams, though it may require more time to see the speed benefits as the team grows in confidence and capability.

Measuring Team Performance

Measuring the performance and speed of your team is essential for continuous improvement. **Key Performance Indicators (KPIs)** such as task completion rates, project cycle times, and customer satisfaction scores can provide insights into team efficiency. Tracking these metrics over time helps identify trends and areas needing attention.

Productivity metrics like output per hour or the number of completed tasks per week can also be useful. These metrics provide a clear picture of how much work is being done and how quickly.

Feedback mechanisms such as regular performance reviews, surveys, and team meetings allow for continuous dialogue about performance. This feedback can highlight strengths and areas for improvement, helping teams to adjust their strategies and maintain high-speed performance.

Overcoming Challenges

Building a high-speed team comes with its challenges. **Resistance to change** is common, as people are often comfortable with established routines. To overcome this, leaders should involve team members in the change process, communicate the benefits clearly, and provide training and support.

Skill gaps can also hinder speed. Identifying these gaps and offering targeted training can help bridge them. Encouraging a culture of continuous learning ensures that team members are always developing their skills.

Maintaining **morale** in a high-speed environment can be challenging. It's important to recognize and reward achievements, provide opportunities for growth, and ensure that workloads are manageable. Encouraging teamwork and open communication can also help maintain a positive and motivated team.

Future Trends

Emerging trends and future developments will likely impact how teams are built and managed. **Advancements in technology** such as AI and machine learning are expected to play a significant role in automating routine tasks and optimizing workflows, enabling teams to focus on more strategic activities.

Changes in **work culture**, such as the increasing prevalence of remote work, require new tools and practices for maintaining team cohesion and efficiency. Technologies that support seamless collaboration and communication will be crucial in this evolving work environment.

New methodologies like **Agile** and **Lean** practices will continue to influence team building. These approaches emphasize flexibility, iterative progress, and continuous improvement, which are essential for high-speed teams to adapt quickly to changing demands.

Interactive Elements

To help readers evaluate and improve their team dynamics, consider adding interactive elements such as:

- **Self-Assessment Tools**: Provide questionnaires to evaluate team strengths and areas for improvement.
- **Checklists**: Offer actionable steps to build and maintain a high-speed team.
- **Quizzes**: Assess understanding and application of team-building concepts discussed in the chapter.

These interactive tools can engage readers and provide personalized insights into their team-building practices.

Expert Interviews

Including interviews with experts in team building and leadership can add depth and credibility to the content. For instance, an interview with a renowned leadership coach or a successful project manager can provide valuable insights into effective strategies and real-world applications. Experts can share their experiences, discuss emerging trends, and offer practical advice on building high-speed teams.

Building a high-speed team is a multifaceted process that involves recruiting the right talent, investing in continuous training and development, motivating and engaging team members, and providing effective leadership. By focusing on these elements, you can create a team that not only works quickly but also delivers high-quality results.

As we continue this journey, the next chapters will delve into specific strategies and techniques to enhance execution speed, ensuring that your team can achieve remarkable results swiftly and effectively. With practical advice, personal anecdotes, and thought-provoking insights, this book aims to be your guide to turbocharging your team's execution speed. So, let's continue this exciting journey together and unlock the full potential of your team's speed and efficiency.

Chapter 4

Chapter 4

Streamlining Processes for Maximum Efficiency

In the quest to enhance execution speed, streamlining processes is a critical factor. Efficient processes reduce waste, eliminate bottlenecks, and enable teams to work at their highest potential. This chapter explores how to identify and streamline processes to achieve maximum efficiency and speed.

Identifying Inefficiencies

The first step in streamlining processes is to identify inefficiencies. These inefficiencies can come in many forms, such as redundant steps, bottlenecks, or outdated practices. To pinpoint these issues, start by mapping out your existing workflows. Visualizing the entire process can help you see where delays and inefficiencies occur.

For example, consider a company that recently analyzed its order fulfillment process. They discovered that the approval steps for order processing were causing significant delays. By mapping out the workflow, they identified that some approvals were redundant and could be consolidated. This insight allowed them to streamline the process and reduce fulfillment time.

Eliminating Bottlenecks

Bottlenecks are specific points in a process where work gets delayed or slowed down. Addressing these bottlenecks is essential for improving execution speed. Once you've identified the bottlenecks, analyze their causes. Is it due to insufficient resources, unclear roles, or outdated technology?

A common example of a bottleneck is a single approval point that causes delays in project completion. By decentralizing decision-making or implementing automated approval systems, you can alleviate this bottleneck and speed up the process. For instance, implementing a digital approval system that allows team members to approve requests from their mobile devices can reduce delays caused by waiting for physical signatures.

Standardizing Procedures

Standardizing procedures helps ensure consistency and efficiency across processes. When everyone follows the same procedures, it reduces variability and the likelihood of errors. Develop and document standard operating procedures (SOPs) for key processes. These SOPs should include step-by-step instructions, best practices, and clear guidelines.

For example, a marketing team might create a standardized procedure for content creation that includes steps for research, drafting, editing, and approval. This standardization ensures that each piece of content is produced consistently and efficiently, with fewer errors and less time spent on revisions.

Leveraging Technology

Technology can play a significant role in streamlining processes. Automating repetitive tasks, integrating systems, and using advanced tools can enhance efficiency and speed. Invest in technology that aligns with your team's needs and supports your workflow.

For instance, project management software can automate task assignments, track progress, and provide real-time updates. Collaboration tools like Slack or Microsoft Teams facilitate quick communication and information sharing. By leveraging these technologies, you can reduce manual work and accelerate process completion.

Personal Story: The Power of Process Improvement

In a previous role, I was involved in a project to streamline our product development process. We started by mapping out the entire workflow and identifying inefficiencies. One major issue was the lengthy review process, which involved multiple departments and resulted in delays.

We implemented a new system that allowed for simultaneous reviews and feedback. This change significantly reduced the time required for reviews and sped up the overall development process. The project was completed ahead of schedule, and the streamlined process was adopted for future projects. This experience demonstrated the transformative impact of process improvement on execution speed.

Quotes and References

To emphasize the importance of process streamlining, consider the words of W. Edwards Deming, a pioneer in quality management: "If you can't describe what you are doing as a process, you don't know what you're doing." This quote highlights the importance of understanding and optimizing processes to achieve efficiency.

A report by McKinsey & Company found that companies that streamline processes and adopt best practices are 30% more likely to achieve operational excellence. This statistic underscores the significant benefits of process optimization in driving efficiency and speed.

Thought-Provoking Questions

Reflect on these questions as you consider streamlining your processes: What steps in your current workflows are causing delays? How can you eliminate or automate these steps? What technology or tools could enhance your process efficiency? Answering these questions can help you identify areas for improvement and implement effective strategies.

Exercises and Activities

Conduct a process mapping exercise with your team. Identify a key workflow and map out each step. Discuss potential inefficiencies and brainstorm solutions to streamline the process. This exercise will provide valuable insights and foster a collaborative approach to process improvement.

Analogies and Metaphors

Streamlining processes is like tuning a musical instrument. Just as a well-tuned instrument produces a clear and harmonious sound, a streamlined process ensures smooth and efficient workflow. By fine-tuning each step and eliminating unnecessary elements, you achieve optimal performance and speed.

Case Studies

To understand how to streamline processes, let's look at real-world examples of organizations that have done this successfully. **Toyota** is a prime example. Toyota's approach to streamlining processes, known as the Toyota Production System, focuses on eliminating waste and optimizing every step of production. By continuously improving their processes, Toyota has achieved remarkable efficiency and high-quality output.

Another example is **Amazon**. Amazon has streamlined its supply chain processes to ensure fast delivery and efficient operations. They use advanced data analytics and automation to optimize their inventory management and shipping processes. This allows them to process and ship orders quickly, meeting customer demands effectively.

Tools and Technologies

Various tools and technologies can help streamline processes. **Workflow automation software** like **Zapier** or **Integromat** can automate repetitive tasks, freeing up time for more strategic activities. These tools connect different applications and automate workflows, reducing manual effort and minimizing errors.

Process mapping tools like **Lucidchart** or **Microsoft Visio** help visualize processes and identify areas for improvement. By mapping out each step, teams can see where bottlenecks occur and develop strategies to streamline the workflow.

Data analytics platforms like **Tableau** or **Power BI** provide insights into process performance. These tools analyze data from various sources, offering a clear picture of how processes are functioning and where improvements can be made.

Leadership's Role

Leadership plays a crucial role in driving process improvement initiatives. Effective leaders foster a culture of continuous improvement, encouraging team members to identify inefficiencies and suggest solutions. By promoting open communication and collaboration, leaders empower their teams to take ownership of process improvements.

Leaders should lead by example, demonstrating a commitment to efficiency and quality. By making swift decisions and removing obstacles, leaders can help teams implement changes quickly and effectively. Additionally, providing training and resources ensures that team members have the skills and tools needed to optimize processes.

Measuring Efficiency

Measuring the efficiency of your processes is essential for continuous improvement. **Key Performance Indicators (KPIs)** such as cycle time, throughput, and defect rates provide insights into process performance. Tracking these metrics helps identify trends and areas needing attention.

Process metrics like lead time, process completion rate, and resource utilization offer a detailed view of process efficiency. These metrics help teams understand how well their processes are functioning and where improvements are needed.

Feedback mechanisms such as regular performance reviews, surveys, and team meetings allow for continuous dialogue about process performance. This feedback helps identify strengths and areas for improvement, guiding teams in their efforts to streamline workflows.

Overcoming Resistance

Streamlining processes often faces resistance to change. People are comfortable with established routines, and changes can be seen as disruptive. To overcome this resistance, involve team members in the change process, communicate the benefits clearly, and provide training and support. Addressing concerns and providing opportunities for team members to voice their opinions can help gain buy-in. Encouraging a culture of continuous improvement, where changes are seen as opportunities for growth rather than threats, can also help overcome resistance.

Future Trends

Emerging trends and future developments will likely impact how processes are streamlined. **Advancements in technology** such as AI and machine learning are expected to play a significant role in automating routine tasks and optimizing workflows. These technologies can analyze large amounts of data, identifying inefficiencies and suggesting improvements.

Changes in **work culture**, such as the increasing prevalence of remote work, require new tools and practices for maintaining process efficiency. Technologies that support seamless collaboration and communication will be crucial in this evolving work environment.

New methodologies like **Lean** and **Six Sigma** will continue to influence process improvement practices. These approaches emphasize efficiency, quality, and continuous improvement, which are essential for streamlining processes.

Interactive Elements

To help readers evaluate and improve their processes, consider adding interactive elements such as:

- **Self-Assessment Tools**: Provide questionnaires to evaluate process strengths and areas for improvement.
- **Checklists**: Offer actionable steps to streamline processes.

- **Quizzes**: Assess understanding and application of process improvement concepts discussed in the chapter.

These interactive tools can engage readers and provide personalized insights into their process improvement practices.

Expert Interviews

Including interviews with experts in process improvement can add depth and credibility to the content. For instance, an interview with a Six Sigma Black Belt or a Lean expert can provide valuable insights into effective strategies and real-world applications. Experts can share their experiences, discuss emerging trends, and offer practical advice on streamlining processes. Streamlining processes is essential for achieving maximum efficiency and speed. By identifying inefficiencies, eliminating bottlenecks, standardizing procedures, and leveraging technology, you create a streamlined workflow that enhances execution speed. In the next chapters, we will explore specific techniques and strategies to further boost your team's performance and drive successful outcomes.

With practical advice, personal anecdotes, and thought-provoking insights, this book aims to be your guide to turbocharging your team's execution speed. Let's continue this journey together and unlock the full potential of your team's efficiency and effectiveness.

Chapter 5

Chapter 5

Enhancing Communication for Speed

Effective communication is the lifeblood of any high-speed team. When communication flows smoothly, team members are aligned, informed, and able to execute tasks swiftly. In this chapter, we will delve into strategies for enhancing communication within your team to maximize execution speed. We'll explore the role of clarity, technology, feedback, and team dynamics in fostering effective communication.

The Role of Clarity in Communication

Clarity is the cornerstone of effective communication. Ambiguity and miscommunication can lead to errors, delays, and confusion. To ensure clarity, it is essential to communicate goals, expectations, and instructions in a straightforward and precise manner. This involves being specific about what needs to be done, by whom, and by when.

For example, when assigning tasks, clearly define the objectives, deadlines, and any relevant details. Instead of saying, "Please work on this report soon," specify, "Please complete the quarterly sales report by 5 PM on Friday, including the sales figures for Q2 and Q3." This level of detail reduces the likelihood of misunderstandings and ensures that everyone is on the same page.

Leveraging Technology for Efficient Communication

Technology plays a crucial role in facilitating efficient communication. Modern tools and platforms can streamline information sharing, enhance collaboration, and keep everyone informed in real time. Implement communication tools such as Slack, Microsoft Teams, or Asana to manage conversations, track progress, and share updates.

For instance, using a project management tool allows team members to post updates, ask questions, and share files in a centralized location. This reduces the need for lengthy email threads and ensures that everyone has access to the latest information. Additionally, video conferencing tools like Zoom or Google Meet can facilitate real-time discussions and decision-making, especially for remote or distributed teams.

The Importance of Feedback

Feedback is a vital component of effective communication. Regular feedback helps team members understand their performance, identify areas for improvement, and make necessary adjustments. Constructive feedback should be specific, actionable, and delivered in a timely manner.

In my experience managing teams, I found that implementing a structured feedback process, such as weekly one-on-one meetings or feedback surveys, significantly improved communication and performance. Team members appreciated the opportunity to receive guidance and make improvements, which ultimately enhanced overall execution speed.

Fostering Open Communication

Encouraging open communication is key to creating a collaborative and high-speed team environment. Team members should feel comfortable sharing ideas, asking questions, and raising concerns without fear of judgment or reprisal. Foster an environment where feedback is welcomed and valued.

Consider implementing regular team meetings or brainstorming sessions where everyone has the opportunity to contribute. An open-door policy, where team members are encouraged to approach leadership with their thoughts and concerns, can also promote a culture of transparency and trust.

Personal Story: The Power of Open Dialogue

At one point, I led a project team that was experiencing communication breakdowns, leading to delays and frustration. To address this, we implemented a weekly team meeting where each member could share their progress, challenges, and ideas. We also encouraged an open-feedback culture, where team members could voice their opinions and suggest improvements.

This approach not only improved communication but also fostered a sense of collaboration and unity. Team members felt more engaged and motivated, and we saw a significant improvement in execution speed and project outcomes. This experience reinforced the importance of open and transparent communication in achieving high performance.

Quotes and References

Consider the words of management expert Peter Drucker: "The most important thing in communication is hearing what isn't said." This quote highlights the significance of understanding and addressing underlying issues and concerns in communication. Effective communication involves not just conveying information but also listening and responding to the needs and feedback of team members.

A study by McKinsey & Company found that companies with effective communication practices experience 25% higher productivity and 30% higher employee satisfaction. This underscores the direct impact of communication on team performance and overall success.

Thought-Provoking Questions

As you reflect on enhancing communication within your team, consider these questions: How clear are your current communication practices? What technologies can you implement to improve information sharing and collaboration? How can you foster a culture of open and constructive feedback? Reflecting on these questions can help you identify areas for improvement and develop strategies to enhance communication.

Exercises and Activities

Conduct a communication audit with your team. Review current communication practices and tools, and gather feedback on their effectiveness. Identify any gaps or areas for improvement, and develop an action plan to address these issues. This exercise will provide valuable insights and help you implement strategies for better communication.

Analogies and Metaphors

Enhancing communication is like tuning a radio to find the clearest signal. Just as you need to adjust the dial to get a clear and uninterrupted broadcast, effective communication requires fine-tuning and adjustment to ensure that messages are clear and understood by everyone.

Case Studies

To illustrate the importance of maintaining quality while increasing speed, let's look at some real-world examples. **Apple** is a prime example of a company that balances speed and quality. Despite the rapid pace of innovation in the tech industry, Apple consistently delivers high-quality products by adhering to stringent quality control processes and continuously improving its production techniques.

Another example is **Toyota**. Toyota's lean manufacturing principles focus on producing high-quality products efficiently. By implementing continuous improvement practices (Kaizen) and involving every team member in quality assurance, Toyota ensures that speed does not compromise the quality of its vehicles.

Tools and Technologies

Several tools and technologies can help maintain quality while increasing speed. **Quality management software** like **SAP Quality Management** or **Qualityze** provides tools for tracking and improving quality throughout the production process. These platforms offer features like real-time quality monitoring, defect tracking, and compliance management.

Automated testing tools such as **Selenium** or **Jenkins** are crucial in software development. These tools automate the testing process, ensuring that new features are thoroughly tested for quality without slowing down the development cycle.

Collaboration platforms like **Asana** or **Trello** help teams coordinate tasks and maintain quality standards. These tools provide visibility into project progress and enable team members to collaborate effectively, ensuring that quality is maintained throughout the project lifecycle.

Leadership's Role

Leadership plays a crucial role in maintaining quality while increasing speed. Effective leaders set clear quality standards and communicate the importance of quality to their teams. They foster a culture of accountability, where team members take ownership of quality and strive for continuous improvement.

Leaders should also lead by example, demonstrating a commitment to quality in their actions and decisions. By providing the necessary resources and support, leaders can empower their teams to achieve high-quality results quickly.

Measuring Quality

Measuring quality is essential to ensure that speed does not compromise standards. **Key Performance Indicators (KPIs)** such as defect rates, customer satisfaction scores, and return rates provide insights into product quality. Tracking these metrics helps identify trends and areas needing attention.

Process metrics like error rates, rework levels, and first-pass yield offer a detailed view of quality performance. These metrics help teams understand how well their processes are functioning and where improvements are needed.

Feedback mechanisms such as regular performance reviews, customer surveys, and team meetings allow for continuous dialogue about quality performance. This feedback helps identify strengths and areas for improvement, guiding teams in their efforts to maintain high-quality standards.

Overcoming Challenges

Maintaining quality while increasing speed often faces challenges such as resource constraints, skill gaps, and resistance to change. To overcome these obstacles, involve team members in the quality improvement process, provide training and support, and communicate the benefits of maintaining quality standards.

Addressing concerns and providing opportunities for team members to voice their opinions can help gain buy-in. Encouraging a culture of continuous improvement, where changes are seen as opportunities for growth rather than threats, can also help overcome resistance.

Future Trends

Emerging trends and future developments will likely impact how quality is maintained while increasing speed. **Advancements in technology** such as AI and machine learning are expected to play a significant role in automating quality assurance processes. These technologies can analyze large amounts of data, identifying defects and suggesting improvements.

Changes in **work culture**, such as the increasing prevalence of remote work, require new tools and practices for maintaining quality standards. Technologies that support seamless collaboration and communication will be crucial in this evolving work environment.

New methodologies like **Lean Six Sigma** will continue to influence quality improvement practices. These approaches emphasize efficiency, quality, and continuous improvement, which are essential for maintaining quality while increasing speed.

Interactive Elements

To help readers evaluate and improve their quality standards, consider adding interactive elements such as:

- **Self-Assessment Tools**: Provide questionnaires to evaluate quality strengths and areas for improvement.

- **Checklists**: Offer actionable steps to maintain quality standards.

- **Quizzes**: Assess understanding and application of quality improvement concepts discussed in the chapter.

These interactive tools can engage readers and provide personalized insights into their quality improvement practices.

Expert Interviews

Including interviews with experts in quality management can add depth and credibility to the content. For instance, an interview with a Six Sigma Black Belt or a Total Quality Management (TQM) expert can provide valuable insights into effective strategies and real-world applications. Experts can share their experiences, discuss emerging trends, and offer practical advice on maintaining quality while increasing speed.

Effective communication is essential for enhancing execution speed and overall team performance. By ensuring clarity, leveraging technology, providing regular feedback, and fostering open dialogue, you create an environment where communication supports swift and efficient execution. In the following chapters, we will explore additional strategies and techniques to further boost your team's speed and success.

With practical advice, personal anecdotes, and thought-provoking insights, this book aims to be your guide to turbocharging your team's execution speed. Let's continue this journey together and unlock the full potential of your team's communication and performance.

Chapter 6

Chapter 6

Developing a Results-Driven Culture

Creating a results-driven culture is essential for achieving high execution speed and overall success. In a results-driven culture, the focus is on achieving goals and delivering outcomes efficiently and effectively. This chapter will explore how to develop and nurture such a culture within your team or organization, including setting clear goals, fostering accountability, celebrating successes, and encouraging continuous improvement.

Setting Clear and Achievable Goals

The foundation of a results-driven culture is the establishment of clear and achievable goals. Goals provide direction, motivation, and a measure of progress. To set effective goals, use the SMART criteria—Specific, Measurable, Achievable, Relevant, and Time-bound. This framework ensures that goals are well-defined and attainable.

For instance, rather than setting a vague goal like "increase sales," set a specific goal such as "increase quarterly sales by 15% by the end of the next quarter." This goal is clear, measurable, achievable, relevant to the business, and bound by a timeframe. By setting such precise goals, you provide a clear target for your team to aim for, which enhances focus and execution speed.

Fostering Accountability

Accountability is crucial in a results-driven culture. When team members are held accountable for their performance, they are more likely to take ownership of their tasks and strive to meet their goals. Establish clear expectations and responsibilities for each team member, and ensure that they understand how their individual contributions impact the overall success of the team.

Implement regular performance reviews and check-ins to monitor progress and provide feedback. For example, holding bi-weekly progress meetings can help keep everyone on track and address any issues promptly. When team members are accountable, they are more motivated to achieve results and contribute to the team's success.

Celebrating Successes

Recognizing and celebrating successes is an important aspect of fostering a results-driven culture. Celebrating achievements boosts morale, reinforces positive behavior, and motivates team members to continue striving for excellence. Acknowledge both individual and team accomplishments, and celebrate milestones along the way.

For example, consider implementing a monthly recognition program where outstanding achievements are highlighted, or organize team celebrations for reaching significant milestones. Celebrations don't have to be elaborate; even a simple acknowledgment during a team meeting or a thank-you note can go a long way in boosting morale and reinforcing a results-driven mindset.

Encouraging Continuous Improvement

A results-driven culture is also characterized by a commitment to continuous improvement.

Encourage team members to seek out opportunities for learning and development, and support them in their efforts to enhance their skills and knowledge. Promote a mindset of experimentation and innovation, where team members are encouraged to test new approaches and learn from their experiences.

Incorporate regular feedback loops and review processes to evaluate performance and identify areas for improvement. For example, conducting post-project reviews to analyze what worked well and what could be improved can provide valuable insights for future projects. By fostering a culture of continuous improvement, you ensure that your team remains adaptable and capable of achieving even higher levels of performance.

Personal Story: Building a Results-Driven Team

I once led a project team that was struggling with meeting deadlines and achieving targets. To address this, we implemented a results-driven approach by setting clear goals, establishing accountability measures, and celebrating our successes. We set specific targets for each project phase, tracked progress closely, and recognized team members for their contributions.

As a result, the team became more focused and motivated, and we significantly improved our execution speed and project outcomes. Celebrating our achievements and providing regular feedback helped us stay aligned with our goals and continuously strive for better results. This experience demonstrated the transformative impact of developing a results-driven culture on team performance.

Quotes and References

Consider the words of business guru Jim Collins: "Great companies are built by people who are passionate about achieving great results." This quote emphasizes the importance of passion and dedication in achieving results and building a high-performing team.

A study by Gallup found that organizations with a strong results-driven culture experience 22% higher profitability and 21% higher productivity. This statistic highlights the significant benefits of fostering a results-driven culture in driving organizational success.

Thought-Provoking Questions

As you work on developing a results-driven culture, reflect on these questions: What specific goals can you set to drive your team's performance? How can you enhance accountability and ownership among team members? What strategies can you implement to recognize and celebrate successes? Reflecting on these questions can help you identify key actions to foster a results-driven culture.

Exercises and Activities

Conduct a goal-setting workshop with your team. Discuss and define specific, measurable, achievable, relevant, and time-bound goals for your projects or initiatives. Develop a plan for tracking progress and providing regular feedback. This workshop will help align the team's efforts with clear objectives and foster a results-driven mindset.

Analogies and Metaphors

Developing a results-driven culture is like tuning a high-performance sports car. Just as a sports car requires precise adjustments and maintenance to achieve peak performance, a results-driven culture requires clear goals, accountability, and continuous improvement to drive success. By fine-tuning these elements, you ensure that your team operates at its highest potential.

Case Studies

To illustrate the importance of fostering a culture of speed, let's look at some real-world examples. **Netflix** is a prime example of a company that has built a culture of speed. By encouraging innovation and quick decision-making, Netflix has been able to rapidly adapt to market changes and deliver new content quickly. Their "Freedom and Responsibility" culture empowers employees to make decisions swiftly, without excessive red tape.

Another example is **SpaceX**. SpaceX's culture emphasizes rapid iteration and continuous improvement. By embracing a fail-fast philosophy, they quickly learn from their mistakes and make the necessary adjustments. This approach has enabled them to achieve significant advancements in space technology in a relatively short time.

Tools and Technologies

Several tools and technologies can support a culture of speed. **Agile project management tools** like **JIRA** or **Trello** facilitate quick iterations and adaptations by providing a flexible framework for managing projects. These tools help teams stay organized and focused, enabling them to respond quickly to changes.

Communication platforms such as **Slack** or **Microsoft Teams** enhance real-time collaboration and decision-making. These tools reduce the time spent on lengthy email chains and enable instant communication, helping teams move faster.

Workflow automation tools like **Zapier** or **Automate.io** can streamline routine tasks, allowing team members to focus on more strategic activities. Automating repetitive processes reduces bottlenecks and speeds up workflows.

Leadership's Role

Leadership is crucial in fostering a culture of speed. Leaders set the tone by modeling quick decision-making and encouraging a sense of urgency. They must create an environment where team members feel empowered to act swiftly and take calculated risks.

Effective leaders also remove obstacles that hinder speed, such as unnecessary bureaucracy or slow approval processes. By providing clear direction and support, leaders can ensure that teams have the resources they need to move quickly and efficiently.

Measuring Speed

Measuring speed is essential to understand how well the culture of speed is being implemented. **Key Performance Indicators (KPIs)** such as cycle time, time to market, and response time provide insights into how quickly tasks are completed. Tracking these metrics helps identify areas where speed can be improved.

Process metrics like lead time, throughput, and velocity offer a detailed view of speed performance. These metrics help teams understand how well their processes are functioning and where adjustments are needed to enhance speed.

Feedback mechanisms such as regular performance reviews, team meetings, and customer surveys allow for continuous dialogue about speed performance. This feedback helps identify strengths and areas for improvement, guiding teams in their efforts to foster a culture of speed.

Overcoming Resistance

Fostering a culture of speed often faces resistance to change. People may be comfortable with established routines and skeptical of new approaches. To overcome this resistance, involve team members in the change process, communicate the benefits clearly, and provide training and support.

Addressing concerns and providing opportunities for team members to voice their opinions can help gain buy-in. Encouraging a culture of continuous improvement, where changes are seen as opportunities for growth rather than threats, can also help overcome resistance.

Future Trends

Emerging trends and future developments will likely impact how a culture of speed is fostered. **Advancements in technology** such as AI and machine learning are expected to play a significant role in automating decision-making processes. These technologies can analyze large amounts of data quickly, enabling faster and more informed decisions.

Changes in **work culture**, such as the increasing prevalence of remote work, require new tools and practices for maintaining speed. Technologies that support seamless collaboration and communication will be crucial in this evolving work environment.

New methodologies like **Lean Startup** will continue to influence how speed is fostered. These approaches emphasize rapid experimentation and validated learning, which are essential for fostering a culture of speed.

Interactive Elements

To help readers evaluate and improve their speed culture, consider adding interactive elements such as:

- **Self-Assessment Tools**: Provide questionnaires to evaluate strengths and areas for improvement in fostering a culture of speed.
- **Checklists**: Offer actionable steps to enhance speed culture.
- **Quizzes**: Assess understanding and application of speed culture concepts discussed in the chapter.

These interactive tools can engage readers and provide personalized insights into their efforts to foster a culture of speed.

Expert Interviews

Including interviews with experts in fostering a culture of speed can add depth and credibility to the content. For instance, an interview with a thought leader in agile methodologies or a successful entrepreneur can provide valuable insights into effective strategies and real-world applications. Experts can share their experiences, discuss emerging trends, and offer practical advice on fostering a culture of speed.

Developing a results-driven culture is essential for achieving high execution speed and overall success. By setting clear goals, fostering accountability, celebrating successes, and encouraging continuous improvement, you create an environment where performance is prioritized, and results are achieved efficiently. In the following chapters, we will explore additional strategies and techniques to further enhance your team's execution speed and drive successful outcomes.

With practical advice, personal anecdotes, and thought-provoking insights, this book aims to be your guide to turbocharging your team's execution speed. Let's continue this journey together and unlock the full potential of your team's performance and success.

Chapter 7

Chapter 7

Empowering Teams for Speed and Success

Empowering your team is a fundamental element in accelerating execution speed and achieving success. When team members are empowered, they are more engaged, motivated, and capable of making decisions that drive results. This chapter will explore strategies for empowering your team, including fostering autonomy, providing support, encouraging innovation, and building trust.

Fostering Autonomy

Empowering teams begins with fostering autonomy. When team members have the freedom to make decisions and take ownership of their work, they are more likely to be proactive and efficient. Autonomy allows individuals to apply their expertise and creativity to solve problems and achieve goals.

To foster autonomy, clearly define roles and responsibilities, and provide the necessary resources and support for team members to perform their tasks effectively. For instance, instead of micromanaging every detail, allow team members to develop their own solutions and approaches. This not only speeds up execution but also builds confidence and expertise within the team.

Providing Support and Resources

While autonomy is important, it is equally crucial to provide the necessary support and resources. Empowered teams need access to tools, training, and guidance to perform their tasks effectively. Ensure that team members have the skills and knowledge required for their roles and offer ongoing support to address any challenges they may encounter.

Consider implementing regular training sessions or workshops to keep your team updated on the latest tools and techniques relevant to their work. Additionally, providing access to resources such as industry best practices, mentorship, and technical support can help team members overcome obstacles and enhance their performance.

Encouraging Innovation

Innovation is a key driver of execution speed and success. Empowered teams are more likely to experiment with new ideas and approaches, leading to creative solutions and improvements. Encourage a culture of innovation by promoting experimentation and supporting risk-taking.

Create an environment where team members feel safe to propose and test new ideas without fear of failure. For example, implement an idea-sharing platform or regular brainstorming sessions where team members can present and discuss their innovative ideas. Recognize and reward creativity and experimentation to reinforce a culture of innovation.

Building Trust and Collaboration

Trust and collaboration are essential components of an empowered team. When team members trust each other and work collaboratively, they are more likely to communicate effectively, share knowledge, and support one another. Building trust involves being transparent, reliable, and supportive.

Foster collaboration by encouraging open communication and teamwork. Implement team-building activities and create opportunities for team members to work together on projects. For instance, organizing cross-functional teams for specific projects can help build relationships and enhance collaboration across different areas of expertise.

Personal Story: Empowering a High-Performing Team

In one of my previous roles, I led a project where empowering the team was crucial for success. We were working on a complex initiative with tight deadlines, and it was essential for the team to act quickly and make decisions independently. I provided clear goals and guidelines but allowed the team the freedom to determine the best approach to achieve those goals.

The team thrived under this autonomy, and their innovative solutions and proactive problem-solving significantly accelerated the project's progress. Regular check-ins and support ensured that they had the resources they needed, and the collaborative environment fostered a strong sense of trust and commitment. This experience highlighted the positive impact of empowerment on team performance and execution speed.

Quotes and References

Consider the words of management consultant and author Patrick Lencioni: "The single greatest advantage of a team is its ability to learn faster than the competition." This quote underscores the importance of empowering teams to make decisions and innovate, which leads to faster learning and improved performance.

A study by Harvard Business Review found that organizations with empowered teams experience 22% higher employee engagement and 25% higher productivity. This statistic highlights the significant benefits of team empowerment in driving success and efficiency.

Thought-Provoking Questions

Reflect on these questions as you work on empowering your team: How can you provide more autonomy and decision-making power to your team members? What resources and support do they need to succeed? How can you foster a culture of innovation and collaboration? Answering these questions can help you develop strategies to empower your team effectively.

Exercises and Activities

Conduct an empowerment workshop with your team. Discuss ways to increase autonomy, provide support, and encourage innovation. Develop an action plan to implement these strategies and set up a system for regular feedback and assessment. This workshop will help align your team's efforts with the principles of empowerment and enhance their performance.

Analogies and Metaphors

Empowering a team is like giving a garden the right conditions to grow. Just as a garden needs sunlight, water, and nutrients to flourish, a team needs autonomy, support, and resources to thrive. By providing the right environment, you enable your team to grow, innovate, and achieve exceptional results.

Case Studies

To illustrate the importance of evaluating and refining execution speed, let's look at some real-world examples. **Amazon** is a prime example of a company that continuously evaluates and refines its execution speed. Amazon uses data-driven decision-making to constantly improve its delivery times and customer service. By analyzing performance metrics and customer feedback, Amazon identifies areas for improvement and implements changes swiftly.

Another example is **General Electric (GE)**, particularly during the tenure of former CEO Jack Welch. GE's commitment to Six Sigma methodologies helped the company streamline its operations, reduce defects, and enhance efficiency. By rigorously measuring performance and refining processes, GE achieved significant improvements in execution speed.

Tools and Technologies

Several tools and technologies can support the evaluation and refinement of execution speed. **Data analytics platforms** like **Tableau** or **Power BI** enable organizations to visualize and analyze performance metrics. These tools help teams identify trends, pinpoint inefficiencies, and make data-driven decisions to improve speed.

Performance management software such as **Workday** or **BambooHR** can track employee performance and productivity. These platforms provide insights into individual and team performance, helping leaders understand how well their teams are executing tasks and where improvements are needed.

Project management tools like **Asana** or **JIRA** offer features for tracking project timelines, task completion rates, and team collaboration. These tools help ensure that projects stay on schedule and that execution speed is optimized.

Leadership's Role

Leadership plays a crucial role in evaluating and refining execution speed. Leaders must create a culture of continuous improvement, where regular evaluation and refinement are part of the organizational routine. By encouraging open communication and feedback, leaders can gain insights into what is working well and what needs improvement.

Effective leaders also provide the necessary resources and support for evaluation and refinement efforts. This includes investing in tools and technologies, offering training and development opportunities, and fostering a mindset of adaptability and growth within their teams.

Measuring Progress

Measuring progress is essential to understand how well execution speed is being improved. **Key Performance Indicators (KPIs)** such as project completion time, cycle time, and throughput provide insights into how quickly tasks are being completed. Tracking these metrics helps identify areas where speed can be enhanced.

Process metrics like defect rates, rework levels, and first-pass yield offer a detailed view of process efficiency. These metrics help teams understand how well their processes are functioning and where adjustments are needed to enhance speed.

Feedback mechanisms such as regular performance reviews, team meetings, and customer surveys allow for continuous dialogue about speed performance. This feedback helps identify strengths and areas for improvement, guiding teams in their efforts to refine execution speed.

Overcoming Challenges

Evaluating and refining execution speed often faces challenges such as resource constraints, resistance to change, and maintaining morale. To overcome these obstacles, involve team members in the evaluation process, communicate the benefits clearly, and provide training and support.

Addressing concerns and providing opportunities for team members to voice their opinions can help gain buy-in. Encouraging a culture of continuous improvement, where changes are seen as opportunities for growth rather than threats, can also help overcome resistance.

Future Trends

Emerging trends and future developments will likely impact how execution speed is evaluated and refined. **Advancements in technology** such as AI and machine learning are expected to play a significant role in automating performance evaluation processes. These technologies can analyze large amounts of data quickly, enabling faster and more informed decisions.

Changes in **work culture**, such as the increasing prevalence of remote work, require new tools and practices for maintaining speed. Technologies that support seamless collaboration and communication will be crucial in this evolving work environment.

New methodologies like **Lean Startup** will continue to influence how speed is evaluated and refined. These approaches emphasize rapid experimentation and validated learning, which are essential for continuous improvement.

Interactive Elements

To help readers evaluate and refine their execution speed, consider adding interactive elements such as:

- **Self-Assessment Tools**: Provide questionnaires to evaluate strengths and areas for improvement in execution speed.

- **Checklists**: Offer actionable steps to enhance speed.

- **Quizzes**: Assess understanding and application of speed improvement concepts discussed in the chapter.

These interactive tools can engage readers and provide personalized insights into their efforts to refine execution speed.

Expert Interviews

Including interviews with experts in evaluating and refining execution speed can add depth and credibility to the content. For instance, an interview with a Six Sigma Black Belt or a Total Quality Management (TQM) expert can provide valuable insights into effective strategies and real-world applications. Experts can share their experiences, discuss emerging trends, and offer practical advice on refining execution speed.

Empowering your team is essential for accelerating execution speed and achieving success. By fostering autonomy, providing support and resources, encouraging innovation, and building trust, you create an environment where team members are motivated, engaged, and capable of driving results. In the next chapters, we will explore additional strategies and techniques to further enhance your team's performance and success.

With practical advice, personal anecdotes, and thought-provoking insights, this book aims to be your guide to turbocharging your team's execution speed. Let's continue this journey together and unlock the full potential of your team's performance and success.

Chapter 8

Chapter 8

Mastering Time Management for Speed and Efficiency

Effective time management is a critical factor in enhancing execution speed and achieving efficiency. By mastering time management, you can ensure that tasks are completed on schedule, resources are utilized effectively, and team members remain productive. This chapter will delve into strategies for mastering time management, including prioritizing tasks, avoiding procrastination, optimizing workflows, and balancing work and life.

Prioritizing Tasks

The ability to prioritize tasks effectively is essential for managing time and boosting execution speed. Prioritization involves identifying the most important tasks that will drive progress towards your goals and focusing on those tasks first. This ensures that you are working on activities that have the greatest impact and avoiding time spent on less critical tasks.

To prioritize tasks, use techniques such as the Eisenhower Matrix, which categorizes tasks into four quadrants: urgent and important, important but not urgent, urgent but not important, and neither urgent nor important. This framework helps you focus on tasks that are both urgent and important while planning for those that are important but not urgent. By organizing tasks in this way, you can allocate your time more effectively and prevent important activities from being overlooked.

Avoiding Procrastination

Procrastination can be a major barrier to effective time management and execution speed. Delaying tasks can lead to missed deadlines, increased stress, and lower productivity. To overcome procrastination, identify the underlying reasons for delay and implement strategies to address them.

One effective approach is the Pomodoro Technique, which involves breaking tasks into short, manageable intervals (usually 25 minutes) followed by a short break. This technique helps maintain focus and makes large tasks seem less daunting. Additionally, setting specific deadlines and breaking tasks into smaller steps can help create a sense of urgency and make it easier to start working on them.

Optimizing Workflows

Optimizing workflows is another key aspect of time management. Streamlining processes and eliminating inefficiencies can significantly improve execution speed and productivity. Evaluate your current workflows to identify areas for improvement and implement changes to enhance efficiency.

For example, automating repetitive tasks using tools and software can save time and reduce the risk of errors. Implementing standardized procedures and using project management tools to track progress and coordinate activities can also help streamline workflows. Regularly reviewing and refining your processes ensures that your workflows remain effective and aligned with your goals.

Balancing Work and Life

Maintaining a balance between work and personal life is crucial for long-term efficiency and well-being. Overworking can lead to burnout and decreased productivity, while a healthy work-life balance helps sustain energy levels and motivation. To achieve this balance, set clear boundaries between work and personal time and prioritize self-care.

Establish a routine that includes time for relaxation, hobbies, and social activities. For example, scheduling regular breaks throughout the day and setting aside time for exercise or leisure activities can help recharge your energy and prevent burnout. By maintaining a healthy balance, you ensure that you remain productive and engaged in both your professional and personal life.

Personal Story: Time Management Success

In a previous role, I was managing multiple projects with tight deadlines and competing priorities. To effectively manage my time, I implemented a prioritization system using the Eisenhower Matrix and adopted the Pomodoro Technique for focused work sessions. I also optimized workflows by automating repetitive tasks and using project management software to track progress.

By applying these time management strategies, I was able to improve my productivity and meet deadlines consistently. Balancing work with regular breaks and personal time helped me avoid burnout and maintain a high level of performance. This experience demonstrated the impact of effective time management on achieving success and maintaining efficiency.

Quotes and References

Consider the words of time management expert Brian Tracy: "Time management is not a static system but a dynamic, ongoing process of continually adjusting to meet your goals and objectives." This quote emphasizes the importance of continually refining time management practices to stay aligned with your goals.

A study by the American Psychological Association found that effective time management is associated with reduced stress and improved job satisfaction. This statistic highlights the benefits of mastering time management for both personal well-being and professional success.

Thought-Provoking Questions

As you work on mastering time management, reflect on these questions: How can you better prioritize your tasks to enhance productivity? What strategies can you implement to overcome procrastination? How can you optimize your workflows to improve efficiency? Reflecting on these questions can help you identify key areas for improvement and develop effective time management strategies.

Exercises and Activities

Conduct a time management audit with your team. Review current practices and identify areas for improvement. Implement time management techniques such as prioritization, the Pomodoro Technique, and workflow optimization. Develop an action plan to address procrastination and balance work and personal life. This audit will provide valuable insights and help you implement strategies for better time management.

Analogies and Metaphors

Mastering time management is like tuning a high-performance engine. Just as a well-tuned engine runs smoothly and efficiently, effective time management ensures that your tasks and activities are executed with precision and efficiency. By fine-tuning your time management practices, you optimize your performance and achieve your goals more effectively.

Case Studies

To understand the importance of maintaining and sustaining high execution speed, let's look at some real-world examples. **Toyota** is known for its lean manufacturing and continuous improvement practices, which have helped maintain high execution speed over decades. By fostering a culture of Kaizen (continuous improvement), Toyota ensures that its processes are always optimized for speed and efficiency.

Another example is **Netflix**, which has managed to sustain rapid innovation and delivery speed in the highly competitive entertainment industry. Netflix maintains its execution speed by continuously evaluating its content delivery methods, investing in technology, and encouraging a culture of agility and flexibility.

Tools and Technologies

Various tools and technologies can help sustain high execution speed. **Performance monitoring tools** like **New Relic** or **Datadog** provide real-time insights into system performance, helping teams quickly identify and resolve issues that could slow down execution.

Continuous integration and continuous deployment (CI/CD) tools such as **Jenkins** or

GitLab help maintain high execution speed in software development. These tools automate the testing and deployment processes, allowing for faster and more reliable releases.

Collaboration tools like **Slack** or **Microsoft Teams** facilitate seamless communication among team members, ensuring that everyone is on the same page and that tasks are completed quickly.

Leadership's Role

Leadership plays a crucial role in maintaining high execution speed. Leaders must continuously reinforce the importance of speed and efficiency within their teams. This involves setting clear expectations, providing regular feedback, and recognizing and rewarding fast and efficient performance.

Effective leaders also create an environment that supports sustained high speed. This includes providing the necessary resources, fostering a culture of continuous improvement, and encouraging innovation. By leading by example and demonstrating a commitment to speed, leaders can inspire their teams to maintain high execution levels.

Measuring Long-Term Success

To ensure that high execution speed is sustained, it's important to measure long-term success. **Key Performance Indicators (KPIs)** such as on-time delivery rates, customer satisfaction scores, and productivity metrics provide insights into how well execution speed is being maintained.

Longitudinal studies and **trend analysis** can help identify patterns and areas for improvement over time. By regularly reviewing these metrics, teams can ensure that they are not only maintaining speed but also improving efficiency and effectiveness.

Overcoming Challenges

Sustaining high execution speed comes with its own set of challenges, such as burnout, resource depletion, and maintaining quality. To overcome these challenges, it's essential to promote a healthy work-life balance and ensure that team members have the necessary support and resources.

Encouraging regular breaks, offering professional development opportunities, and providing a supportive work environment can help prevent burnout and maintain morale. Additionally, continuous monitoring and adjustment of workloads can ensure that resources are used efficiently without compromising quality.

Future Trends

Emerging trends and future developments will influence how high execution speed is maintained. **Artificial intelligence (AI)** and **machine learning** are expected to play a significant role in automating routine tasks and optimizing processes, allowing teams to maintain high speed with less effort.

Remote work and **flexible work arrangements** will continue to impact how teams operate and maintain speed. Technologies that support remote collaboration and virtual project management will be essential in this evolving work landscape.

New methodologies and frameworks, such as **Agile** and **DevOps**, will continue to influence how teams sustain high execution speed. These approaches emphasize flexibility, continuous feedback, and rapid iteration, which are crucial for maintaining speed.

Interactive Elements

To help readers sustain high execution speed, consider adding interactive elements such as:

- **Self-Assessment Tools**: Provide questionnaires to evaluate how well they are maintaining speed.

- **Checklists**: Offer actionable steps to sustain high execution speed.

- **Quizzes**: Assess understanding and application of concepts discussed in the chapter.

These interactive tools can engage readers and provide personalized insights into their efforts to maintain high execution speed.

Expert Interviews

Including interviews with experts in sustaining high execution speed can add depth and credibility to the content. For instance, an interview with a lean manufacturing expert or a productivity consultant can provide valuable insights into effective strategies and real-world applications. Experts can share their experiences, discuss emerging trends, and offer practical advice on maintaining high execution speed.

Mastering time management is essential for enhancing execution speed and achieving efficiency. By prioritizing tasks, avoiding procrastination, optimizing workflows, and balancing work and personal life, you create a foundation for success and productivity. In the next chapters, we will explore additional strategies and techniques to further enhance your team's performance and drive successful outcomes.

With practical advice, personal anecdotes, and thought-provoking insights, this book aims to be your guide to turbocharging your team's execution speed. Let's continue this journey together and unlock the full potential of effective time management.

Conclusion

Conclusion

Accelerating Success Through Execution Speed

As we reach the end of our journey together, it's clear that the path to accelerating success is paved with effective strategies and a commitment to continuous improvement. This book has explored various facets of enhancing execution speed, from setting clear goals and fostering a results-driven culture to mastering time management and empowering your team.

The Power of Execution Speed

Execution speed is not merely a measure of how quickly tasks are completed; it reflects the agility, efficiency, and effectiveness of your entire operation. It encompasses the ability to prioritize tasks, make swift decisions, and adapt to changing circumstances. By focusing on execution speed, you position yourself and your team to respond more effectively to opportunities and challenges, driving success and achieving your objectives more efficiently.

Implementing Key Strategies

Throughout this book, we've discussed numerous strategies to boost execution speed. Setting clear and achievable goals provides direction and focus, while a results-driven culture fosters accountability and celebrates achievements. Mastering time management helps in prioritizing tasks and optimizing workflows, and empowering your team encourages autonomy and innovation. Each of these strategies plays a crucial role in enhancing your overall performance and achieving your goals.

Commitment to Continuous Improvement

Success is not a destination but a continuous journey. Embracing a mindset of continuous improvement is vital for sustaining and enhancing execution speed. Regularly review your processes, seek feedback, and be open to new ideas and approaches. By committing to ongoing development and adaptation, you ensure that you and your team remain at the forefront of performance and efficiency.

The Role of Leadership

Effective leadership is at the heart of accelerating execution speed. Leaders who inspire, support, and empower their teams create an environment where high performance and innovation thrive. Your role as a leader involves setting clear expectations, providing the necessary resources, and fostering a culture that values results and continuous improvement. By leading with purpose and commitment, you drive your team toward greater success and achievement.

Encouraging Reflection and Action

As you conclude your journey through this book, take time to reflect on the insights and strategies discussed. Consider how you can apply these principles to your own work and team dynamics. Identify areas where you can improve and implement the techniques that resonate most with your goals and challenges. By taking proactive steps and applying what you've learned, you'll be well-equipped to enhance your execution speed and drive meaningful results.

Final Thoughts

Accelerating execution speed is about more than just completing tasks quickly; it's about achieving excellence and driving success through effective strategies, empowered teams, and a commitment to continuous improvement. By embracing the principles outlined in this book, you set the stage for achieving remarkable results and reaching your goals with efficiency and agility.

Thank you for embarking on this journey with me. I hope this book has provided valuable insights and practical advice to help you accelerate your path to success. Remember, the pursuit of excellence is a continuous process, and the strategies you've learned here are tools to help you navigate that path with confidence and effectiveness.

Here's to your success and the exciting journey ahead!

Appendix

Appendix

Additional Resources and Tools for Enhancing Execution Speed

This appendix provides supplementary resources and tools to further support your journey toward enhancing execution speed. It includes recommended reading, useful tools, templates, and additional exercises that can help you implement the strategies discussed in the book.

Recommended Reading

1. **"The 7 Habits of Highly Effective People" by Stephen R. Covey**
   This classic book offers timeless advice on

personal effectiveness and time management, providing valuable insights into setting priorities and achieving goals.

2. **"Deep Work: Rules for Focused Success in a Distracted World" by Cal Newport**
   Newport explores the concept of deep work and how to cultivate focused, productive work habits that accelerate execution speed and efficiency.

3. **"Atomic Habits: An Easy & Proven Way to Build Good Habits & Break Bad Ones" by James Clear**
   Clear's book delves into the science of habit formation and how small changes can lead to significant improvements in productivity and performance.

4. **"Drive: The Surprising Truth About What Motivates Us" by Daniel H. Pink**
   This book examines the science of motivation and how understanding what drives individuals can enhance team performance and execution speed.

Useful Tools and Software

1. **Trello**
   A visual project management tool that

helps in organizing tasks, tracking progress, and managing workflows. Trello's boards, lists, and cards make it easy to visualize and prioritize tasks.

2. **Asana**
   A project management platform that facilitates task assignment, progress tracking, and collaboration among team members. Asana is ideal for managing complex projects and maintaining accountability.

3. **Slack**
   A communication tool that enhances team collaboration and information sharing. Slack's channels and direct messaging features streamline communication and reduce email overload.

4. **Evernote**
   A note-taking app that helps in capturing ideas, organizing notes, and managing tasks. Evernote's tagging and search features make it easy to access important information quickly.

5. **RescueTime**
   A time-tracking tool that provides insights into how time is spent on various

activities. RescueTime helps identify time-wasting habits and optimize productivity.

Templates and Worksheets

1. **Goal Setting Worksheet**
   Use this template to define SMART goals for your projects or initiatives. The worksheet guides you through specifying, measuring, achieving, and timing your goals.

2. **Prioritization Matrix Template**
   This tool helps categorize tasks into urgent and important categories. Use it to prioritize your tasks and focus on what matters most.

3. **Time Management Planner**
   A daily or weekly planner template designed to help you organize your schedule, set priorities, and manage your time effectively.

4. **Feedback and Improvement Log**
   Track feedback received and areas for improvement. This log helps in recording insights from performance reviews and planning actions for continuous development.

Additional Exercises and Activities

1. **Time Management Audit**
   Conduct a time management audit by analyzing how you currently spend your time and identifying areas for improvement. Use the insights to develop a plan for better time management.

2. **Brainstorming Session**
   Organize a brainstorming session with your team to generate innovative ideas and solutions. Use techniques such as mind mapping or the SCAMPER method to stimulate creativity.

3. **Goal Review and Adjustment**
   Regularly review your goals and progress. Use this exercise to adjust your goals based on changing priorities or new insights.

4. **Team-Building Activities**
   Engage in team-building exercises to strengthen collaboration and trust within your team. Activities such as problem-solving challenges or team workshops can enhance teamwork and communication.

Glossary of Terms

- **Execution Speed:** The ability to complete tasks and achieve goals efficiently and effectively.

- **SMART Goals:** A framework for setting goals that are Specific, Measurable, Achievable, Relevant, and Time-bound.

- **Pomodoro Technique:** A time management method that involves working in short intervals (typically 25 minutes) followed by a short break.

- **Prioritization Matrix:** A tool for categorizing tasks based on their urgency and importance to determine what to focus on first.

Additional Resources

- **Project Management Institute (PMI):** Offers certifications, resources, and guidelines for project management professionals. Website

- **Harvard Business Review (HBR):** Provides articles and research on business management, leadership, and productivity. Website

- **TED Talks:** Explore TED Talks on productivity, leadership, and time management for additional insights and inspiration. Website

Final Thoughts

The resources and tools provided in this appendix are designed to complement the strategies discussed in the book and support your journey toward enhanced execution speed and efficiency. By utilizing these resources, you can further refine your skills, optimize your processes, and achieve greater success in your personal and professional endeavors.

References

References

1. Covey, Stephen R. *The 7 Habits of Highly Effective People: Powerful Lessons in Personal Change.* Free Press, 1989. This foundational book on personal effectiveness offers timeless principles for managing time, setting priorities, and achieving goals.

2. Newport, Cal. *Deep Work: Rules for Focused Success in a Distracted World.* Grand Central Publishing, 2016. Newport explores the concept of deep work and provides practical advice on

cultivating focused and productive work habits.

3. Clear, James. *Atomic Habits: An Easy & Proven Way to Build Good Habits & Break Bad Ones.* Avery, 2018.
Clear's book delves into the science of habit formation and how small, incremental changes can lead to significant improvements in productivity.

4. Pink, Daniel H. *Drive: The Surprising Truth About What Motivates Us.* Riverhead Books, 2009.
Pink examines the science of motivation and how understanding what drives individuals can enhance performance and team dynamics.

5. Tracy, Brian. *Time Management: Proven Techniques for Making Every Minute Count.* AMACOM, 2007.
Tracy's book offers practical time management strategies and techniques to improve productivity and effectiveness.

6. American Psychological Association. "Time Management and Stress." *American Psychologist*, vol. 58, no. 3, 2003, pp. 185-190.
This article provides insights into the

relationship between time management and stress, highlighting the benefits of effective time management.

7. Lencioni, Patrick. *The Five Dysfunctions of a Team: A Leadership Fable.* Jossey-Bass, 2002.
Lencioni's book explores common issues that hinder team performance and provides strategies for building a cohesive and high-performing team.

8. Drucker, Peter F. *The Effective Executive: The Definitive Guide to Getting the Right Things Done.* HarperBusiness, 1966.
Drucker's classic work on effective management emphasizes the importance of focusing on results and prioritizing tasks to achieve success.

9. Allen, David. *Getting Things Done: The Art of Stress-Free Productivity.* Penguin Books, 2001.
Allen's book presents a comprehensive time management system designed to help individuals and teams achieve productivity and reduce stress.

10. Harvard Business Review. "How to Manage Your Time." *Harvard Business Review*, vol. 92, no. 7, 2014, pp. 114-121.

This article provides practical advice and techniques for managing time effectively in a business context.

11. Goleman, Daniel. *Emotional Intelligence: Why It Can Matter More Than IQ*. Bantam Books, 1995. Goleman's book explores the concept of emotional intelligence and its impact on personal and professional success.

12. Peters, Tom, and Robert H. Waterman Jr. *In Search of Excellence: Lessons from America's Best-Run Companies*. Harper & Row, 1982. Peters and Waterman examine the practices and principles that contribute to the success of leading companies, offering valuable lessons for enhancing performance.

13. Carnegie, Dale. *How to Win Friends and Influence People*. Simon & Schuster, 1936. Carnegie's classic work on interpersonal skills provides timeless advice on building relationships and influencing others effectively.

14. Kotter, John P. *Leading Change*. Harvard Business Review Press, 1996. Kotter's book outlines a proven framework for leading organizational change and achieving successful outcomes.

15. Duhigg, Charles. *The Power of Habit: Why We Do What We Do in Life and Business.* Random House, 2012.
Duhigg explores the science of habit formation and how understanding habits can lead to improved productivity and success.

16. Peters, Tom. *The Circle of Innovation: You Can't Shrink Your Way to Greatness.* Alfred A. Knopf, 1997.
Peters discusses the importance of innovation and how organizations can foster a culture of creativity and change.

17. Christensen, Clayton M. *The Innovator's Dilemma: When New Technologies Cause Great Firms to Fail.* Harvard Business Review Press, 1997.
Christensen examines why successful companies often fail to adapt to disruptive innovations and provides insights on overcoming this challenge.

18. Anderson, Chris. *The Long Tail: Why the Future of Business Is Selling Less of More.* Hyperion, 2006.
Anderson's book explores the concept of the "long tail" and its implications for business strategy and market trends.

19. Meyer, Christopher. *The End of the Suburbs: Where the American Dream Is Moving.* St. Martin's Press, 2013.
Meyer examines changing trends in suburban living and their impact on business and lifestyle.

20. Sinek, Simon. *Start with Why: How Great Leaders Inspire Everyone to Take Action.* Penguin Books, 2009.
Sinek's book focuses on the importance of understanding and communicating the purpose behind actions and leadership.

www.ingramcontent.com/pod-product-compliance
Lightning Source LLC
Chambersburg PA
CBHW050301230526
45471CB00005B/1965